WAR HISTORIES

THE GULF WAR

BY ALEX MONROE

TORQUE™

BELLWETHER MEDIA ★ MINNEAPOLIS, MN

Torque brims with excitement perfect for thrill-seekers of all kinds. Discover daring survival skills, explore uncharted worlds, and marvel at mighty engines and extreme sports. In *Torque* books, anything can happen. Are you ready?

This edition first published in 2025 by Bellwether Media, Inc.

Library of Congress Cataloging-in-Publication Data

LC record for The Gulf War available at: https://lccn.loc.gov/2024035384

Editor: Rebecca Sabelko Designer: Josh Brink

Printed in the United States of America, North Mankato, MN.

TABLE OF CONTENTS

WHAT WAS THE GULF WAR?

The Gulf War lasted from 1990 to 1991. It started after Iraq **invaded** Kuwait. The war was a major worldwide conflict. It was the first major conflict after the **Cold War**.

IRAQ INVADING KUWAIT

★ GULF WAR MAP ★

The United States led the effort against Iraq. It sent troops to help. Many other countries sent help, too. This **coalition** included more than 30 countries.

OWING MONEY

In 1990, the **dictator** Saddam Hussein ruled Iraq. The country had just finished a war against Iran in 1988. It now owed Kuwait and many other countries money.

IRAN-IRAQ WAR

★ IRAQI LEADER ★

NAME
Saddam Hussein

NATIONALITY
Iraqi

RANK
President of Iraq (1979 to 2003)

IMPORTANT ACTIONS

- August 2, 1990: Invaded Kuwait
- January 15, 1991: Remained in Kuwait against UN orders
- February 28, 1991: Agreed to stop fighting

Hussein decided to invade Kuwait. He wanted control of its large oil fields. They were worth a lot of money. They would pay off Iraq's **debt**. He also wanted to gain more power in the area.

DESERT SHIELD

On August 2, 1990, Iraq invaded Kuwait. U.S. officials were worried Iraq might move into Saudi Arabia, too.

U.S. TROOPS TRAINING DURING OPERATION DESERT SHIELD

MANY TROOPS

More than 500,000 U.S. troops were in Desert Shield.

★ U.S. LEADER ★

NAME
George H. W. Bush

NATIONALITY
American

RANK
U.S. President (1989 to 1993)

IMPORTANT ACTIONS

- August 7, 1990: Began Operation Desert Shield
- January 17, 1991: Began Operation Desert Storm
- February 28, 1991: Agreed to stop fighting

U.S. President George H. W. Bush sent troops to Saudi Arabia on August 7. He wanted to stop Iraq from gaining power. The U.S. and other countries formed a coalition. These actions were called Operation Desert Shield.

On November 29, the **United Nations** (UN) told Iraq to leave Kuwait by January 15, 1991. The UN would allow action against Iraq if it did not leave.

THE UN ON NOVEMBER 29, 1990

U.S. OFFICIALS ON JANUARY 15, 1991

U.S. officials quickly began making a plan. They aimed to beat Iraq with a fast attack. January 15 came. But Iraq did not leave Kuwait.

DESERT STORM

On January 17, 1991, coalition troops began an air attack. It was called Operation Desert Storm. The U.S. used Hellfire **missiles**. They took out Iraq's air **defenses**.

Coalition aircraft entered Kuwait. They destroyed supply lines. They attacked military sites. By January 28, coalition forces had won the battle in the air.

HELLFIRE MISSILE

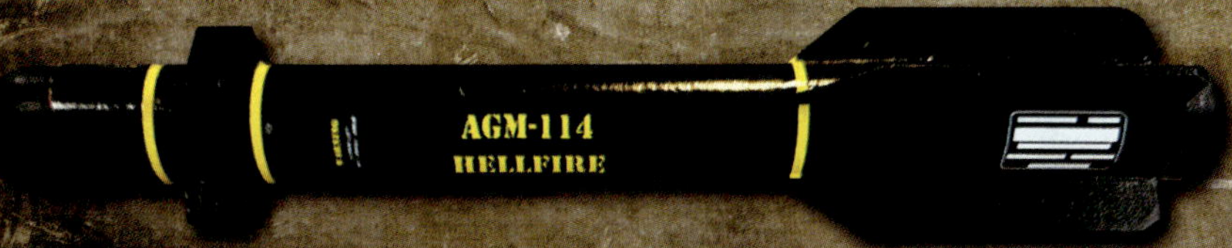

Length:	Weight:	Speed:	Power:
5.3 feet (1.6 meters)	up to 107 pounds (48.5 kilograms)	997 miles (1,605 kilometers) per hour	Can destroy any known tank

DESTROYED AIR BASE

The ground attack began on February 24. This part of the war was called Operation Desert Sabre. Coalition troops quickly rushed into Kuwait.

They attacked Iraqi troops. They planned to push them back into Iraq. Many Iraqi troops quickly **surrendered**. But some fought back. They were quickly beaten.

FAST FIGHT

Operation Desert Sabre ended after just 100 hours!

IRAQI SOLDIERS SURRENDERING

OPERATION DESERT SABRE

Both sides of the fight used tanks. Coalition troops took out the last of Iraq's defenses on February 26. They destroyed many Iraqi tanks. Iraqi troops soon began to leave Kuwait.

On February 27, coalition forces retook the capital of Kuwait. Attacks ended on February 28. The war was over. Kuwait was freed.

★THE WAR AT HOME★

Many people in the U.S. backed the Gulf War. The war was well covered by television news. This may have helped people view the war favorably.

Some Americans spoke out against the war. Thousands of people gathered outside city government buildings. They thought the war was harming too many people.

REBUILDING

Iraqi troops set large oil fields on fire as they left Kuwait. They destroyed most of the country's oil wells. Many troops became sick from the smoke.

The UN placed many orders on Iraq after the war. Iraq had to recognize Kuwait as its own country. It also had to give up larger weapons.

GULF WAR TIMELINE

August 2, 1990
Iraq invades Kuwait

August 7, 1990
Operation Desert Shield begins

November 29, 1990
The UN gives Iraq a deadline to leave Kuwait

KUWAIT OIL FIELD ON FIRE

January 17, 1991
Operation Desert Storm begins

February 28, 1991
The coalition stops its attacks

The war heavily damaged Iraq. Iraq also faced **sanctions** from the UN. It struggled to rebuild. Many people suffered. They had little food or medicine.

U.S. forces stayed in the area after the war. This angered many people in the area. It led to a rise in **extremist groups**. This would draw the U.S. into more wars in the future.

★ BY THE NUMBERS ★

500 people =

MAIN COUNTRIES INVOLVED

- Iraq
- coalition: more than 30 nations including Egypt, Saudi Arabia, the U.K., and the U.S.

TOTAL MILITARY DEATHS

- coalition: around 250 deaths
- Iraq: between 20,000 and 35,000 deaths

CIVILIAN DEATHS

- between 100,000 and 200,000

TOTAL U.S. MILITARY PERSONNEL DEPLOYED

- 694,550

TOTAL U.S. SPENDING

- $72.8 billion (in 2024 dollars)

BOMBS USED IN DESERT STORM

- 88,500 tons (80,286 metric tons)

GLOSSARY

coalition—a joining of groups to work together toward a goal

Cold War—a conflict between the U.S. and the Soviet Union in the second half of the 1900s that did not break out into fighting

debt—the state of owing something, usually money, to someone else

defenses—ways to protect

dictator—a ruler of a country who has total power

extremist groups—people that have strong beliefs that go against the social and moral beliefs of other groups of people; extremist groups may use violence to get what they want.

invaded—entered a land and took control of it

missiles—weapons that travel in the air and explode when they hit a target

sanctions—punishments given to a country for going against international law

surrendered—gave up power or control of something

United Nations—a political group formed in 1945 that works around the world to maintain peace

TO LEARN MORE

AT THE LIBRARY

Elston, Heidi M.D. *George H.W. Bush*. Minneapolis, Minn.: Abdo, 2025.

McKinney, Donna. *Apache Helicopter*. Minneapolis, Minn.: Bellwether Media, 2024.

Monroe, Alex. *The War on Terror*. Minneapolis, Minn.: Bellwether Media, 2025.

ON THE WEB

FACTSURFER

Factsurfer.com gives you a safe, fun way to find more information.

1. Go to www.factsurfer.com
2. Enter "Gulf War" into the search box and click 🔍.
3. Select your book cover to see a list of related content.

INDEX

The images in this book are reproduced through the courtesy of: CW04 J.M. Rodriguez/ NARA & DVIDS, front cover (Iraqi captured tank); SGT. Billings/ NARA & DVIDS, front cover (overturned Iraqi tank); The U.S. National Archives/ NARA & DVIDS, front cover (Iraqi tank on fire); SPEC. Joel Torres/ NARA & DVIDS, front cover (armored equipment background); PHC HOLMES/ Wiki Commons, pp. 2-3, 22-24; r Zymogen92/ Wiki Commons, p. 4; defapress/ Wiki Commons, pp. 6-7; Keystone Pictures USA/ Alamy, p. 7; SSGT. Ruark/ NARA & DVIDS, pp. 8-9; Mark Reinstein, p. 9; Evy Mages/ Getty Images, pp. 10-11; George Bush Presidential Library and Museum, p. 11; SRA Chris Putnam/ NARA & DVIDS, pp. 12-13, 19 (January 17, 1991); DOD Photo/ Alamy, p. 13; Chilion Danforth/ Wiki Commons, p. 13 (Hellfire missile); Johnny Saunderson/ Alamy, pp. 14-15; Langevin Jacques/ Getty Images, p. 15; Pascal Guyot/ Getty Images, pp. 16-17, 17; Mark Reinstein/ Getty Images, p. 17 (war at home feature); Peter Jordan/Popperfoto/ Getty Images, pp. 18-19; SSGT. Lee Corkran/ NARA & DVIDS, p. 18 (August 7, 1990); Maher Attar/ Getty Images, pp. 20-21.